www.finishinglinepress.com

What Is Endured

poems by

Sharon Foley

Finishing Line Press
Georgetown, Kentucky

What Is Endured

Copyright © 2017 by Sharon Foley
ISBN 978-1-63534-103-4 First Edition
All rights reserved under International and Pan-American Copyright Conventions.
No part of this book may be reproduced in any manner whatsoever without written permission from the publisher, except in the case of brief quotations embodied in critical articles and reviews.

ACKNOWLEDGMENTS

Grateful acknowledgment is due to the editors of the following publications in which these poems have appeared, some in slightly different versions.
Chest   "Ophthalmologist"
Creative Wisconsin Magazine   "A Holy Ride with Strangers"
Collecting Life: Poets on Objects Known and Imagined   "Leftovers"
The Aurorean   "I Unfold From my Pocket"

Thank you for the unending support from my husband Lou and sons Sam and Zach and for my talented, steadfast sisters Susan and Judy. To all of my brilliant friends and extended family, as well as the gang at Red Oak Writing who first read most of these poems in some form.

Publisher: Leah Maines

Editor: Christen Kincaid

Cover Art: Public Domain

Author Photo: Jaci Ruben

Cover Design: Elizabeth Maines

Printed in the USA on acid-free paper.
Order online: www.finishinglinepress.com
        also available on amazon.com

Author inquiries and mail orders:
Finishing Line Press
P. O. Box 1626
Georgetown, Kentucky 40324
U. S. A.

Table of Contents

*"The poets work is to put into words those feelings
we all have that are so deep, so important,
and yet so difficult to name . . ."*
—Jane Kenyon

Cardiac Rotation

When they split open your chest
first with curved knife
next serrated saw
both sides held open
with steel surgical spatulas,
I saw inside
the house of your ribs
the ruby muscle's nest
as it pulsed.

When the surgeon
nodded permission,
I dipped my fingers
into the warm
butter of your blood,
slid them along the atrium
firm length of ventricle
until I cradled
that beating hummingbird
in the palm of my hand.

Even as I did this
I knew I wasn't holding you
limp on the table
eyes closed, tongue pushed aside.
Even as the surgeon
stitched you back up
I couldn't forget
your rosebud heart,
beauty beating
just beneath the skin.

I Believed That Night at the VA

Hours of gastric tubes, cardiac compressions,
collapsed on my cot, on call
sleep was prayer
stethoscope a rosary draped around my neck.
When my beeper sounded at 3 a.m.
it was a bugle calling taps.
I called for the room number
found the door that opened
into an irreversible event
like last day on an advent calendar.
I stepped inside
saw green paint, metal bed
a family crouched in the corner.

It could have been any night
inside that yellow linoleum institution
vinegar stench crying my eyes.
But on that night
when I placed my flat drum
on his barreled chest, already cold,
the blue on his lips
as unnatural as witchcraft,
I felt something I never had before.
It was like the rumbling of an approaching train,
rushing closer, whistling louder,
until that moment became more
than sound, or the mottled man
lying still before me,
more than green paint, fluorescent lights,
inconsolable families.

In that sterile laminar air flow room
when I looked up to signal
his heart had given its last,
I felt an expanding communion
with all that remained.

Grief

Stairs to my office
each one Everest
my shoulders swim
in a sea of sweater
rimless reading glasses
two lead telescopes
that teeter on my nose.
All day long
intercoms blare
ring tones startle
my necklace an anchor
that pulls down my head,
and when I
lift it back up
dusk is settling
over Quincy, Illinois
across photos on my walls
both of us
toasting the Red Sea.

After I stack my memos
each one legal-sized
I drive off
to reassemble myself
spread-eagle flat
across your vacant lawn
sink in the grass
until I can't tell
if I'm lying down
or falling up
while I weep
into the flood of night.

Leftovers

I tried to save everything.

I rifled your drawer
sifted through cabinets
gathered bottle caps, ribbons, and bits
tickets, strings, papers,
crumpled receipts from pre-washed jeans
clips from your pin-striped ties
a mountain of scraps.

Things you had touched
I reassembled
into a shadow box,
a display of discards
until I finally saved
even you
inside my porcelain urn.

Tonight I will open the lid
sprinkle my bed
with your ash,
make a sachet of bone-dust
rest it beneath my pillow.

I unfold from my pocket

a square of quilt
that holds your lavender scent
begin my work of stitching
in the quiet kitchen
black coffee, crescent roll
needle weaving in and out
between cotton downy
and plum-colored fabric
as I patch together
this crazy quilt.

I feel rhythm of your breath
remember autumn days
working side by side, quilting
peach cobbler crusts
loaves of braided bread.
This needle
like the movement of my grief
in and out
a pattern never finished.

Ophthalmologist

How many times
have I peered
into black pupils
through the window of lens,
past blue corneas and blooming iris
beyond vitreous chambers
and protein oceans,
until my light reaches
the yellow flush of macula
optic disc, bright as a harvest moon
where nerves and vessels
weave and converge
knitting a synaptic web
where I imagine
all the beautiful
images are stored.

A Holy Ride with Strangers

I squeeze into
this paneled elevator
the door dings shut
closing out the shaft
of light.

I whisper goodbye
to ground level
before we travel up
a carton of strangers
encased together,
satchels, umbrellas, keys
clutched close.

It seems a long time
suspended
hollow tong of cables
thin light, muffled sounds, cold,
like the cold in your chest
that never left.

This elevator shaft seems holy
this small booth
nearly confessional
velvet drapes, hush
a congregation of strangers.

Together we continue
up the chute
until the door dings open
I exit on the twelfth floor
find my mother's room
to say goodbye.

So at Starbucks

when the person in front of you
turns around
and you notice a nodule
protruding from his cheek
it's only natural
you strike up a conversation
about tumors,
since you have one of your own.

You add cream and sugar
until your coffee's just right
sit at a table
and the person tells you his story
that ends with one year to live.
His lower lip trembles
so you know it's true;   reminds you
of the doctor, one month ago,
telling you over coffee
your parents wouldn't survive.
His lip trembled too
the upper one.

You stand to leave Starbucks
hands shaking
as you try to find change
you don't have
for a city bus.
You walk in the rain
to the columbarium
sit on the floor
beneath your parents' shared niche
sip from your cold double espresso
read out loud
from a back-ordered *Reader's Digest*
as if telling a bedside story
the one about the three bears
waiting to feel just right.

The Oncologist's Daughter

I think it's what saved him;
that dark living room
worn leather La-Z-Boy
olive green curtains pulled tight,
crackle sounds,
as needle settled into vinyl.

It wasn't any particular song
but the round sounds
of tenors; Pavarotti, Domingo,
that slackened his rib cage
lulled his breathing.

I think music held answers
he didn't have
at Clarkson Hospital,
as he strung red chemo lines
threaded tubes of fluids and salts
strived to finely tune
his entire ward.

I wanted to go with him
into the songs,
leave the pleading patients
whose voices flooded
our answering machine
at home.

Stomach Cancer
Kansas Internship

I was paged overhead
to room 352
because you were dying.
And when you finished living
your room bleached clean
I was ordered to find your family
explain cancer.

When I tried to speak
into that vacuum of grief
failing to offer reason or comfort,
your children gathered round and held *me* up
like stakes hold peonies in summer
their flowers full
of the weight of bloom
like my head still full of you.

Yesterday I took your vitals
wrapped my blood pressure cuff
around your purple stained arm
so thin it could have been a stem,
while you talked
of jarring gooseberry jam for pie,
knitting plum colored mittens
grandchildren like brass buttons
I tried to feel your pulse.

Each day it was useless
we both knew
fluids in, fluids out
respiratory rates.
Each day your stomach collapsed
further into itself
and you went with it
folding into the seam of your bed,
like pumpkins recede into porches
in November,
after the inner flesh used up
only the stain of pumpkin left.

Day Care

She tells me
what a great day he had;
tottering by the stream
collecting frogs, snails.
What's more,
he learned to tie his shoes,
wash his hands before snack.

I glance at the fat-foam
number pads on the floor,
the bubble-gum colored walls
that wrap this day care of regression.
Each day the alphabet grows shorter
refrains from yesterday's limerick lost
the class is stooped, all Velcro.

I clear my throat
since it's starting to quiver,
and that tick in my neck
is jumping like a fly.
I tell this day-care assistant
more rapidly than I'd like
that this, in fact,
is the second time
he has learned to tie his shoes
that three years ago
he saved people, not frogs.

I begin to babble
about blue cheese and Swiss
he preferred the latter, if aged.
Growing tomatoes, always green,
hunting in Nebraska hail.
I mutter together socks, mitts
from his yellow bear cubby
and she brings him to me, my father
my cheeks wet
mascara everywhere but on my face
despair growing like a beanstalk,
when my father, leans over and asks:
"Who are you?"

That's What It Was

We were planning my mother's garden
which boulder to add to the waterfall
so the stream of water flowed just right.
She worried her Japanese maple
might not survive with the oak shade gone
they had grown together for years.

We discussed these things
on the ninth floor of St. Luke's
seemingly unaware
of the dire situation
overlooking the fact
sick people reside in hospitals
and those intubated in intensive care
like her, the most precarious.

Because she could still laugh
as we played hangman
on a dry erase board,
and she wrote orders
with her one working hand:
'make sure dog is fed'
'take the garbage out'
and I read poems daily at her bedside
even recited from the Complete Book of Duplicate Bridge.
So when she took her last breath
we didn't know   that's what it was.

Full-Count

This morning
deciding on a sweater or coat
oatmeal or cereal
easy enough
but later, at the doctors,
I'll have to decide on Taxol or Taxotere,
lymph node dissection vs. sentinel node,
whether to sign my living will.

It's a whole new ball game
there's no umpire to call me safe
friends and fans have long gone,
best they don't see me
so ill-prepared,
since I'm a rookie.

When You Died

I couldn't make sense of it.
I'm standing in a Hallmark aisle
since I need to express a feeling
and I've heard it's a good place to go.
I'm surrounded by shelves
of bi-fold paper greetings;
bursting with limerick and phrase
Wishing You Well, Thinking of You
Better Luck Next Time.
I loosen my shirt,
since clichés are closing in
and I'm feeling claustrophobic.
I drop my jacket to the floor
hat, scarf, gloves
shoes off
not my socks,
I keep those on.

I sift through racks
of lace-trimmed cards,
pop-up bluebirds
metallic bells that really ring,
gummy hearts,
until I open a laminated pink plastic cover
and it plays the Happy Birthday Song.
Now I can barely breathe
and my socks go too.

Gulfs

That closed music box
oval-shaped
like hazel eyes you squinted.
Looking beyond the stretch
of wheat fields,
waiting for a postmarked letter
from a husband,
gone for years into a war
neither of you asked for
but became what separated
the two of you
along with the Gulf of Thailand.

At night he counted stars
he named one after you.
Daily he counted steps
and bullet shells
falling closer
than any shooting star.
You knew these things
like knowing fool's gold
could scratch a copper penny
or stories your mother read
each night when you were five,
from the red leather book of Aesop's
were only fables.

You can see stars too
in summer, from Kansas,
some have yellowed behind clouds
others fallen.
The letter you never read again
arrived with two soldiers
saluting a kind of bravery
never asked for,
you were already closing the door
when they handed it to you
and you put it inside a music box
on your single dresser.

Waiting Room Amnesia

I've been introduced
to waiting room chairs before,
some leather, others velour
vinyl dread.
All tottering stools
avoided.
Some come prepared;
sudoku to solve, scarves to knit,
others read at the mercy
of another's literary choice.

As I take stock
of my lounging choices,
I notice a mid-century recliner
with cushion-rest for arms
kick-out for legs.
What's more, there's TV
a headset for easy listening.
Even though the pea-green plaid
clashes with my coat,
I'm fevered and weak
settle in for a while
forget why I came
sit   wait

Whatever It Takes

I was already stuffed
with flow-charts and protocols,
'standards of care,'
armed with salves and creams
when my diploma came.
I had shocked hearts, tapped spines
rubber-tubed chests
closed incisions with loops of suture.
I had run the halls of Methodist Hospital
like barebacked steeds
run the Palio, in Siena
when the bells chime noon.

But soon I was shaking rattles
burning incense in my closet
pleading with the armored stars,
casting spells, whatever it took;
the *eye of a newt.*
But the sick died anyway
the bells kept ringing
and I was never able to write my poems.

Post-Op Call

Even
the sound of music
changed
notes off key
everything sharp
or flat.
Reflected light changed
blue sky to a chardonnay,
all chocolate white.
Tongue clumsy in my mouth
breathing on loudspeaker
ears two satellite dish receptors
a telescope for eyes
zooming in on the phone
I was afraid to touch
as if a living thing.
The stillness could have been
a groom before "I do."
Even the sun hesitated
behind the clouds
until the call   "all clear."

42nd and Farnam

How could I have known
when I was five
cleaning house with you
in my paisley skirt
or when you held my hand
as we crossed the street
to school, yellow larks singing,
that twenty years later
I would do the same
for you.

Gladly hold your hand
as you crossed from your bed
to I don't know where,
the only sound was breath
your wrist thin as a bird's spine.

How could I have known
ten years beyond that bedside,
I would still remember you,
when I stood in the narrow
hallway of a school,
or at a street corner
like 42nd and Farnam
trying to cross to safety,
looking for traffic
just like you taught,
first left, then right

then left again.

I Can't Find the Spoons

It's winter now
and snow is lulling
each house in our village.
I've lived longer than I should have
even though it will be
less than you
even though I'm not ready
the house a mess
I can't find the spoons
and the dark clouds
are beautiful in storm
even now as they move
eclipsing the evening sun.

Sharon Foley's poems have received recognition and awards from the Wisconsin Fellowship of Poets, the Wisconsin Regional Writer's Association as well as the Wisconsin Academy of Sciences, *Arts and Letters'* literary magazine. Her poems have appeared in numerous journals, including *The Aurorean, Common Ground Review, White Pelican Review, Bellowing Ark* and *Plainsongs* as well as the anthology, *Collecting Life: Poets on Objects known and Imagined.* This is her first collection of poems.

She lives in Whitefish Bay Wisconsin with her husband, children and ferocious five-pound morkie, Dash. When not writing, she enjoys reading, long walks, crafting and collecting sea glass along the shores of Lake Michigan.

Board certified in Internal Medicine and Dermatology, daughter of an Oncologist, and with personal experience with illness, Sharon has been circling the themes of sickness and mortality in her writing for some time. Her journey has given her a unique perspective on the 'endurance' that life requires, regardless of outcome.

www.ingramcontent.com/pod-product-compliance
Lightning Source LLC
LaVergne TN
LVHW021128080426
835510LV00021B/3356